THIS RECYCLING JOURNAL
BELONGS TO

_____

_____

 'Love Earth'

DATE: _____

How did I Help The Environment Today?

What Can I Re-use?

☐

☐

☐

☐

☐

☐

My Recycling List for Today

Today I Love Earth Because...

How Did I Reduce my Waste Today?

Recycle  'Love Earth'

DATE: _____

How did I Help The Environment Today?

☐

☐

☐

☐

☐

☐

What Can I Re-use?

_____
_____
_____
_____
_____
_____
_____
_____

My Recycling List for Today

_____
_____
_____
_____
_____
_____
_____
_____
_____
_____
_____
_____

Today I Love Earth Because...

_____
_____
_____

How Did I Reduce my Waste Today?

_____
_____
_____
_____
_____

 'Love Earth'

DATE: _____

How did I Help The Environment Today?

What Can I Re-use?

☐

☐

☐

☐

☐

☐

My Recycling List for Today

Today I Love Earth Because...

How Did I Reduce my Waste Today?

Recycle

 'Love Earth'

D A T E : _____

How did I Help The Environment Today?

☐

☐

☐

☐

☐

☐

Today I Love Earth Because...

_____

_____

_____

What Can I Re-use?

_____
_____
_____
_____
_____
_____
_____
_____

My Recycling List for Today

_____
_____
_____
_____
_____
_____
_____
_____
_____
_____
_____

How Did I Reduce my Waste Today?

_____
_____
_____
_____
_____
_____

Recycle 'Love Earth'

DATE: _____

How did I Help The Environment Today?

- [ ]
- [ ]
- [ ]
- [ ]
- [ ]
- [ ]

Today I Love Earth Because...

_____
_____

What Can I Re-use?

_____
_____
_____
_____
_____
_____
_____

My Recycling List for Today

_____
_____
_____
_____
_____
_____
_____
_____
_____
_____

How Did I Reduce my Waste Today?

_____
_____
_____
_____
_____

 'Love Earth'

DATE: _____

How did I Help The Environment Today?

☐

☐

☐

☐

☐

☐

Today I Love Earth Because...

_____
_____
_____

What Can I Re-use?

_____
_____
_____
_____
_____
_____
_____
_____

My Recycling List for Today

_____
_____
_____
_____
_____
_____
_____
_____
_____
_____
_____

How Did I Reduce my Waste Today?

_____
_____
_____
_____
_____

 'Love Earth'

DATE: _____

How did I Help The Environment Today?

☐

☐

☐

☐

☐

☐

Today I Love Earth Because...

_____

_____

What Can I Re-use?

_____
_____
_____
_____
_____
_____
_____

My Recycling List for Today

_____
_____
_____
_____
_____
_____
_____
_____
_____
_____

How Did I Reduce my Waste Today?

_____
_____
_____
_____
_____

Recycle

'Love Earth'

DATE: _____

How did I Help The Environment Today?

- ☐
- ☐
- ☐
- ☐
- ☐
- ☐

What Can I Re-use?

_____
_____
_____
_____
_____
_____
_____
_____

My Recycling List for Today

_____
_____
_____
_____
_____
_____
_____
_____
_____
_____

Today I Love Earth Because...

_____
_____
_____

How Did I Reduce my Waste Today?

_____
_____
_____
_____
_____

Recycle

'Love Earth'

D A T E: _____

How did I Help The Environment Today?

☐

☐

☐

☐

☐

☐

Today I Love Earth Because...

_____
_____
_____

What Can I Re-use?

_____
_____
_____
_____
_____
_____
_____

My Recycling List for Today

_____
_____
_____
_____
_____
_____
_____
_____

How Did I Reduce my Waste Today?

_____
_____
_____
_____
_____

Recycle

 'Love Earth'

DATE: _____

How did I Help The Environment Today?

☐

☐

☐

☐

☐

☐

Today I Love Earth Because...

_____
_____
_____

What Can I Re-use?

_____
_____
_____
_____
_____
_____
_____
_____

My Recycling List for Today

_____
_____
_____
_____
_____
_____
_____
_____
_____

How Did I Reduce my Waste Today?

_____
_____
_____
_____
_____

 'Love Earth'

DATE: _____

How did I Help The Environment Today?

☐

☐

☐

☐

☐

☐

Today I Love Earth Because...

_____

_____

What Can I Re-use?

_____

_____

_____

_____

_____

_____

My Recycling List for Today

_____

_____

_____

_____

_____

_____

_____

_____

How Did I Reduce my Waste Today?

_____

_____

_____

_____

Recycle

'Love Earth'

DATE: _____

How did I Help The Environment Today?

- ☐
- ☐
- ☐
- ☐
- ☐
- ☐

What Can I Re-use?

_____
_____
_____
_____
_____
_____
_____
_____

My Recycling List for Today

_____
_____
_____
_____
_____
_____
_____
_____
_____
_____
_____

Today I Love Earth Because...

_____
_____
_____

How Did I Reduce my Waste Today?

_____
_____
_____
_____
_____

 'Love Earth'

DATE: _____

How did I Help The Environment Today?

What Can I Re-use?

☐

☐

☐

☐

☐

☐

My Recycling List for Today

Today I Love Earth Because...

How Did I Reduce my Waste Today?

 'Love Earth'

DATE: _____

How did I Help The Environment Today?

☐

☐

☐

☐

☐

☐

What Can I Re-use?

_____
_____
_____
_____
_____
_____
_____
_____

My Recycling List for Today

_____
_____
_____
_____
_____
_____
_____
_____
_____
_____

Today I Love Earth Because...

_____
_____
_____

How Did I Reduce my Waste Today?

_____
_____
_____
_____
_____

 'Love Earth'

Recycle

DATE: _____

How did I Help The Environment Today?

What Can I Re-use?

☐

☐

☐

☐

☐

☐

My Recycling List for Today

Today I Love Earth Because...

How Did I Reduce my Waste Today?

 'Love Earth'

DATE: _____

How did I Help The Environment Today?

☐

☐

☐

☐

☐

☐

What Can I Re-use?

_____
_____
_____
_____
_____
_____
_____

My Recycling List for Today

_____
_____
_____
_____
_____
_____
_____
_____
_____
_____

Today I Love Earth Because...

_____
_____
_____

How Did I Reduce my Waste Today?

_____
_____
_____
_____
_____

 'Love Earth'

DATE: _____

How did I Help The Environment Today?

☐

☐

☐

☐

☐

☐

Today I Love Earth Because...

_____
_____

What Can I Re-use?

_____
_____
_____
_____
_____
_____
_____

My Recycling List for Today

_____
_____
_____
_____
_____
_____
_____
_____
_____

How Did I Reduce my Waste Today?

_____
_____
_____
_____
_____

 'Love Earth'

DATE: _____

How did I Help The Environment Today?

What Can I Re-use?

_____
_____
_____
_____
_____
_____
_____

My Recycling List for Today

_____
_____
_____
_____
_____
_____
_____
_____
_____

Today I Love Earth Because...

_____
_____
_____

How Did I Reduce my Waste Today?

_____
_____
_____
_____
_____

Recycle 'Love Earth'

D A T E: _____

How did I Help The Environment Today?

What Can I Re-use?

☐

☐

☐

☐

☐

☐

My Recycling List for Today

Today I Love Earth Because...

How Did I Reduce my Waste Today?

Recycle

'Love Earth'

DATE: _____

How did I Help The Environment Today?

- ☐
- ☐
- ☐
- ☐
- ☐
- ☐

What Can I Re-use?

_____
_____
_____
_____
_____
_____
_____
_____

My Recycling List for Today

_____
_____
_____
_____
_____
_____
_____
_____
_____
_____
_____

Today I Love Earth Because...

_____
_____
_____

How Did I Reduce my Waste Today?

_____
_____
_____
_____
_____

 'Love Earth'

DATE: _____

How did I Help The Environment Today?

☐

☐

☐

☐

☐

☐

What Can I Re-use?

_____
_____
_____
_____
_____
_____
_____

My Recycling List for Today

_____
_____
_____
_____
_____
_____
_____
_____
_____

Today I Love Earth Because...

_____
_____

How Did I Reduce my Waste Today?

_____
_____
_____
_____

 'Love Earth'

DATE: _____

How did I Help The Environment Today?

What Can I Re-use?

☐

☐

☐

☐

☐

☐

My Recycling List for Today

Today I Love Earth Because...

How Did I Reduce my Waste Today?

 'Love Earth'

DATE: _____

How did I Help The Environment Today?

What Can I Re-use?

☐
_____

☐
_____

☐
_____

My Recycling List for Today

☐
_____

☐
_____

☐
_____

Today I Love Earth Because...
_____

_____

_____

How Did I Reduce my Waste Today?

_____
_____
_____
_____

Recycle 'Love Earth'

DATE: _____

How did I Help The Environment Today?

☐

☐

☐

☐

☐

☐

What Can I Re-use?

_____
_____
_____
_____
_____
_____
_____
_____

My Recycling List for Today

_____
_____
_____
_____
_____
_____
_____
_____
_____
_____
_____
_____
_____

Today I Love Earth Because...

_____
_____
_____

How Did I Reduce my Waste Today?

_____
_____
_____
_____
_____

Recycle

'Love Earth'

DATE: _____

How did I Help The Environment Today?

- ☐
- ☐
- ☐
- ☐
- ☐
- ☐

What Can I Re-use?

_____
_____
_____
_____
_____
_____
_____
_____
_____

My Recycling List for Today

_____
_____
_____
_____
_____
_____
_____
_____
_____
_____
_____
_____

Today I Love Earth Because...

_____
_____
_____

How Did I Reduce my Waste Today?

_____
_____
_____
_____

 'Love Earth'

DATE: _____

How did I Help The Environment Today?

☐

☐

☐

☐

☐

☐

What Can I Re-use?

_____
_____
_____
_____
_____
_____
_____

My Recycling List for Today

_____
_____
_____
_____
_____
_____
_____
_____
_____
_____

Today I Love Earth Because...

_____
_____
_____

How Did I Reduce my Waste Today?

_____
_____
_____
_____
_____

Recycle

'Love Earth'

DATE: _____

How did I Help The Environment Today?

☐

☐

☐

☐

☐

☐

Today I Love Earth Because...

_____

_____

What Can I Re-use?

_____
_____
_____
_____
_____
_____
_____

My Recycling List for Today

_____
_____
_____
_____
_____
_____
_____
_____

How Did I Reduce my Waste Today?

_____
_____
_____
_____

 'Love Earth'

DATE: _____

How did I Help The Environment Today?

What Can I Re-use?

_____
_____
_____
_____
_____
_____
_____

☐

☐

☐

My Recycling List for Today

☐

_____
_____
_____
_____
_____
_____
_____
_____
_____
_____
_____
_____
_____

☐

☐

Today I Love Earth Because...

_____
_____
_____

How Did I Reduce my Waste Today?

_____
_____
_____
_____
_____

 'Love Earth'

Recycle

DATE: _____

How did I Help The Environment Today?

☐

☐

☐

☐

☐

☐

Today I Love Earth Because...

_____

_____

What Can I Re-use?

_____
_____
_____
_____
_____
_____
_____

My Recycling List for Today

_____
_____
_____
_____
_____
_____
_____
_____

How Did I Reduce my Waste Today?

_____
_____
_____
_____

 'Love Earth'

DATE: _____

How did I Help The Environment Today?

- [ ]
- [ ]
- [ ]
- [ ]
- [ ]
- [ ]

What Can I Re-use?

_____
_____
_____
_____
_____
_____
_____
_____
_____

My Recycling List for Today

_____
_____
_____
_____
_____
_____
_____
_____
_____
_____
_____
_____

Today I Love Earth Because...

_____
_____
_____

How Did I Reduce my Waste Today?

_____
_____
_____
_____
_____

 'Love Earth'

DATE: _____

How did I Help The Environment Today?

☐

☐

☐

☐

☐

☐

What Can I Re-use?

_____
_____
_____
_____
_____
_____
_____
_____

My Recycling List for Today

_____
_____
_____
_____
_____
_____
_____
_____
_____
_____

Today I Love Earth Because...

_____
_____
_____

How Did I Reduce my Waste Today?

_____
_____
_____
_____

 'Love Earth'

DATE: _____

How did I Help The Environment Today?

☐

☐

☐

☐

☐

☐

What Can I Re-use?

_____
_____
_____
_____
_____
_____
_____

My Recycling List for Today

_____
_____
_____
_____
_____
_____
_____
_____
_____
_____

Today I Love Earth Because...

_____
_____
_____

How Did I Reduce my Waste Today?

_____
_____
_____
_____
_____

Recycle

'Love Earth'

DATE: _____

How did I Help The Environment Today?

☐

☐

☐

☐

☐

☐

Today I Love Earth Because...

_____
_____
_____

What Can I Re-use?

_____
_____
_____
_____
_____
_____
_____

My Recycling List for Today

_____
_____
_____
_____
_____
_____
_____
_____

How Did I Reduce my Waste Today?

_____
_____
_____
_____

Recycle

'Love Earth'

DATE: _____

How did I Help The Environment Today?

- [ ]
- [ ]
- [ ]
- [ ]
- [ ]
- [ ]

What Can I Re-use?

_____
_____
_____
_____
_____
_____
_____
_____

My Recycling List for Today

_____
_____
_____
_____
_____
_____
_____
_____
_____
_____
_____
_____

Today I Love Earth Because...

_____
_____
_____

How Did I Reduce my Waste Today?

_____
_____
_____
_____
_____

 'Love Earth'

Recycle

DATE: _____

How did I Help The Environment Today?

☐

☐

☐

☐

☐

☐

Today I Love Earth Because...

_____
_____
_____

What Can I Re-use?

_____
_____
_____
_____
_____
_____
_____
_____
_____

My Recycling List for Today

_____
_____
_____
_____
_____
_____
_____
_____
_____
_____

How Did I Reduce my Waste Today?

_____
_____
_____
_____

Recycle 'Love Earth'

DATE: _____

How did I Help The Environment Today?

☐

☐

☐

☐

☐

☐

Today I Love Earth Because...

_____

_____

_____

What Can I Re-use?

_____
_____
_____
_____
_____
_____
_____

My Recycling List for Today

_____
_____
_____
_____
_____
_____
_____
_____
_____
_____
_____

How Did I Reduce my Waste Today?

_____
_____
_____
_____

Recycle

'Love Earth'

DATE: _____

How did I Help The Environment Today?

☐

☐

☐

☐

☐

☐

Today I Love Earth Because...

_____
_____
_____

What Can I Re-use?

_____
_____
_____
_____
_____
_____
_____
_____

My Recycling List for Today

_____
_____
_____
_____
_____
_____
_____
_____
_____
_____

How Did I Reduce my Waste Today?

_____
_____
_____
_____

 'Love Earth'

DATE: _____

How did I Help The Environment Today?

What Can I Re-use?

☐

☐

☐

☐

☐

☐

My Recycling List for Today

Today I Love Earth Because...

How Did I Reduce my Waste Today?

 'Love Earth'

DATE: _____

How did I Help The Environment Today?

- [ ]
- [ ]
- [ ]
- [ ]
- [ ]
- [ ]

What Can I Re-use?

_____
_____
_____
_____
_____
_____
_____
_____
_____

My Recycling List for Today

_____
_____
_____
_____
_____
_____
_____
_____
_____

Today I Love Earth Because...

_____
_____

How Did I Reduce my Waste Today?

_____
_____
_____
_____

Recycle

'Love Earth'

DATE: _____

How did I Help The Environment Today?

☐

☐

☐

☐

☐

☐

Today I Love Earth Because...

_____
_____
_____

What Can I Re-use?

_____
_____
_____
_____
_____
_____
_____

My Recycling List for Today

_____
_____
_____
_____
_____
_____
_____
_____
_____
_____
_____

How Did I Reduce my Waste Today?

_____
_____
_____
_____
_____

Recycle

'Love Earth'

DATE: _____

How did I Help The Environment Today?

☐

☐

☐

☐

☐

☐

What Can I Re-use?

_____
_____
_____
_____
_____
_____
_____
_____
_____
_____

My Recycling List for Today

_____
_____
_____
_____
_____
_____
_____
_____
_____
_____

Today I Love Earth Because...

_____
_____
_____

How Did I Reduce my Waste Today?

_____
_____
_____
_____

Recycle

'Love Earth'

DATE: _____

How did I Help The Environment Today?

☐

☐

☐

☐

☐

☐

What Can I Re-use?

_____
_____
_____
_____
_____
_____
_____

My Recycling List for Today

_____
_____
_____
_____
_____
_____
_____
_____
_____
_____
_____
_____

Today I Love Earth Because...

_____
_____
_____

How Did I Reduce my Waste Today?

_____
_____
_____
_____
_____

 'Love Earth'

DATE: _____

How did I Help The Environment Today?

☐

☐

☐

☐

☐

☐

Today I Love Earth Because...

_____

_____

What Can I Re-use?

_____
_____
_____
_____
_____
_____
_____

My Recycling List for Today

_____
_____
_____
_____
_____
_____
_____
_____
_____

How Did I Reduce my Waste Today?

_____
_____
_____
_____

 'Love Earth'

DATE: _____

How did I Help The Environment Today?

☐

☐

☐

☐

☐

☐

What Can I Re-use?

_____
_____
_____
_____
_____
_____
_____
_____

My Recycling List for Today

_____
_____
_____
_____
_____
_____
_____
_____
_____

Today I Love Earth Because...

_____
_____
_____

How Did I Reduce my Waste Today?

_____
_____
_____
_____

Recycle

'Love Earth'

DATE: _____

How did I Help The Environment Today?

☐

☐

☐

☐

☐

☐

Today I Love Earth Because...

_____
_____
_____

What Can I Re-use?

_____
_____
_____
_____
_____
_____
_____

My Recycling List for Today

_____
_____
_____
_____
_____
_____
_____
_____

How Did I Reduce my Waste Today?

_____
_____
_____
_____

 'Love Earth'

DATE: _____

How did I Help The Environment Today?

☐

☐

☐

☐

☐

☐

Today I Love Earth Because...

_____
_____
_____

What Can I Re-use?

_____
_____
_____
_____
_____
_____
_____

My Recycling List for Today

_____
_____
_____
_____
_____
_____
_____
_____
_____
_____

How Did I Reduce my Waste Today?

_____
_____
_____
_____
_____

 'Love Earth'

DATE: _____

How did I Help The Environment Today?

What Can I Re-use?

- [ ]
- [ ]
- [ ]
- [ ]
- [ ]
- [ ]

My Recycling List for Today

Today I Love Earth Because...

How Did I Reduce my Waste Today?

 'Love Earth'

DATE: _____

How did I Help The Environment Today?   What Can I Re-use?

☐

☐   _____
                                            _____
☐   _____
                                            _____
☐   _____
                                            _____
☐   _____

☐   My Recycling List for Today

                                            _____
Today I Love Earth Because...   _____
                                            _____
_____   _____
_____   _____
_____   _____
_____   _____
                                            _____
                                            _____
How Did I Reduce my Waste Today?   _____

_____
_____
_____
_____
_____

Recycle

'Love Earth'

DATE: _____

How did I Help The Environment Today?

☐

☐

☐

☐

☐

☐

Today I Love Earth Because...

_____

_____

_____

What Can I Re-use?

_____

_____

_____

_____

_____

_____

_____

My Recycling List for Today

_____

_____

_____

_____

_____

_____

_____

_____

How Did I Reduce my Waste Today?

_____

_____

_____

_____

_____

Recycle
'Love Earth'

DATE: _____

How did I Help The Environment Today?

- [ ]
- [ ]
- [ ]
- [ ]
- [ ]
- [ ]

What Can I Re-use?

_____
_____
_____
_____
_____
_____
_____
_____

My Recycling List for Today

_____
_____
_____
_____
_____
_____
_____
_____
_____
_____
_____
_____
_____
_____

Today I Love Earth Because...

_____
_____
_____

How Did I Reduce my Waste Today?

_____
_____
_____
_____
_____

Recycle
 'Love Earth'

DATE: _____

How did I Help The Environment Today?

☐

☐

☐

☐

☐

☐

What Can I Re-use?

_____
_____
_____
_____
_____
_____
_____
_____
_____

My Recycling List for Today

_____
_____
_____
_____
_____
_____
_____
_____
_____

Today I Love Earth Because...

_____
_____
_____

How Did I Reduce my Waste Today?

_____
_____
_____
_____

Recycle 'Love Earth'

DATE: _____

How did I Help The Environment Today?

☐

☐

☐

☐

☐

☐

Today I Love Earth Because...

_____
_____
_____

What Can I Re-use?

_____
_____
_____
_____
_____
_____
_____

My Recycling List for Today

_____
_____
_____
_____
_____
_____
_____
_____
_____

How Did I Reduce my Waste Today?

_____
_____
_____
_____

 'Love Earth'

DATE: _____

How did I Help The Environment Today?

What Can I Re-use?

_____
_____
_____
_____
_____
_____
_____
_____

My Recycling List for Today

_____
_____
_____
_____
_____
_____
_____
_____
_____
_____
_____

Today I Love Earth Because...

_____
_____
_____

How Did I Reduce my Waste Today?

_____
_____
_____
_____

 'Love Earth'

DATE: _____

How did I Help The Environment Today?

☐

☐

☐

☐

☐

☐

Today I Love Earth Because...

_____
_____
_____

What Can I Re-use?

_____
_____
_____
_____
_____
_____
_____
_____

My Recycling List for Today

_____
_____
_____
_____
_____
_____
_____
_____
_____
_____
_____
_____

How Did I Reduce my Waste Today?

_____
_____
_____
_____
_____

 'Love Earth'

DATE: _____

How did I Help The Environment Today?

☐

☐

☐

☐

☐

☐

Today I Love Earth Because...

_____
_____
_____

What Can I Re-use?

_____
_____
_____
_____
_____
_____
_____

My Recycling List for Today

_____
_____
_____
_____
_____
_____
_____
_____
_____

How Did I Reduce my Waste Today?

_____
_____
_____
_____

 'Love Earth'

D A T E: _____

How did I Help The Environment Today?

☐

☐

☐

☐

☐

☐

Today I Love Earth Because...

_____

_____

_____

What Can I Re-use?

_____
_____
_____
_____
_____
_____
_____
_____
_____

My Recycling List for Today

_____
_____
_____
_____
_____
_____
_____
_____
_____
_____
_____

How Did I Reduce my Waste Today?

_____
_____
_____
_____
_____

 'Love Earth'

DATE: _____

How did I Help The Environment Today?

☐

☐

☐

☐

☐

☐

Today I Love Earth Because...

_____
_____
_____

What Can I Re-use?

_____
_____
_____
_____
_____
_____
_____

My Recycling List for Today

_____
_____
_____
_____
_____
_____
_____
_____
_____

How Did I Reduce my Waste Today?

_____
_____
_____
_____

 'Love Earth'

DATE: _____

How did I Help The Environment Today?

☐

☐

☐

☐

☐

☐

Today I Love Earth Because...

_____
_____
_____

What Can I Re-use?

_____
_____
_____
_____
_____
_____
_____
_____

My Recycling List for Today

_____
_____
_____
_____
_____
_____
_____
_____
_____
_____

How Did I Reduce my Waste Today?

_____
_____
_____
_____

Recycle 'Love Earth'

DATE: _____

How did I Help The Environment Today?

☐

☐

☐

☐

☐

☐

What Can I Re-use?

_____

_____

_____

_____

_____

_____

_____

_____

_____

My Recycling List for Today

_____

_____

_____

_____

_____

_____

_____

_____

_____

_____

Today I Love Earth Because...

_____

_____

_____

How Did I Reduce my Waste Today?

_____

_____

_____

_____

Recycle

'Love Earth'

DATE: _____

How did I Help The Environment Today?

☐

☐

☐

☐

☐

☐

Today I Love Earth Because...

_____
_____
_____

What Can I Re-use?

_____
_____
_____
_____
_____
_____
_____

My Recycling List for Today

_____
_____
_____
_____
_____
_____
_____
_____
_____
_____

How Did I Reduce my Waste Today?

_____
_____
_____
_____
_____

 'Love Earth'

DATE: _____

How did I Help The Environment Today?

☐

☐

☐

☐

☐

☐

What Can I Re-use?

_____
_____
_____
_____
_____
_____
_____

My Recycling List for Today

_____
_____
_____
_____
_____
_____
_____
_____
_____
_____
_____

Today I Love Earth Because...

_____
_____
_____

How Did I Reduce my Waste Today?

_____
_____
_____
_____

 'Love Earth'

DATE: _____

How did I Help The Environment Today?

☐

☐

☐

☐

☐

☐

What Can I Re-use?

_____
_____
_____
_____
_____
_____
_____

My Recycling List for Today

_____
_____
_____
_____
_____
_____
_____
_____
_____

Today I Love Earth Because...

_____
_____
_____

How Did I Reduce my Waste Today?

_____
_____
_____
_____

Recycle 'Love Earth'

DATE: _____

How did I Help The Environment Today?

- [ ]
- [ ]
- [ ]
- [ ]
- [ ]
- [ ]

What Can I Re-use?

_____
_____
_____
_____
_____
_____
_____

My Recycling List for Today

_____
_____
_____
_____
_____
_____
_____
_____
_____

Today I Love Earth Because...

_____
_____
_____

How Did I Reduce my Waste Today?

_____
_____
_____
_____

 'Love Earth'

DATE: _____

How did I Help The Environment Today?

☐

☐

☐

☐

☐

☐

Today I Love Earth Because...

What Can I Re-use?

_____
_____
_____
_____
_____
_____
_____
_____

My Recycling List for Today

_____
_____
_____
_____
_____
_____
_____
_____
_____
_____

How Did I Reduce my Waste Today?

_____
_____
_____
_____

Recycle  'Love Earth'

DATE: _____

How did I Help The Environment Today?

☐

☐

☐

☐

☐

☐

Today I Love Earth Because...

_____
_____
_____

What Can I Re-use?

_____
_____
_____
_____
_____
_____
_____

My Recycling List for Today

_____
_____
_____
_____
_____
_____
_____
_____
_____
_____

How Did I Reduce my Waste Today?

_____
_____
_____
_____
_____

Recycle

'Love Earth'

DATE: _____

How did I Help The Environment Today?

☐

☐

☐

☐

☐

☐

What Can I Re-use?

_____
_____
_____
_____
_____
_____
_____
_____

My Recycling List for Today

_____
_____
_____
_____
_____
_____
_____
_____
_____
_____
_____

Today I Love Earth Because...

_____
_____
_____

How Did I Reduce my Waste Today?

_____
_____
_____
_____

Recycle

'Love Earth'

DATE: _____

How did I Help The Environment Today?

☐

☐

☐

☐

☐

☐

Today I Love Earth Because...

_____
_____
_____

What Can I Re-use?

_____
_____
_____
_____
_____
_____
_____
_____

My Recycling List for Today

_____
_____
_____
_____
_____
_____
_____
_____
_____
_____

How Did I Reduce my Waste Today?

_____
_____
_____
_____

Recycle

'Love Earth'

DATE: _____

How did I Help The Environment Today?

☐

☐

☐

☐

☐

☐

Today I Love Earth Because...

_____

_____

_____

What Can I Re-use?

_____
_____
_____
_____
_____
_____
_____
_____

My Recycling List for Today

_____
_____
_____
_____
_____
_____
_____
_____
_____
_____
_____

How Did I Reduce my Waste Today?

_____
_____
_____
_____

 'Love Earth'

DATE: _____

How did I Help The Environment Today?

- ☐
- ☐
- ☐
- ☐
- ☐
- ☐

What Can I Re-use?

_____
_____
_____
_____
_____
_____
_____
_____

My Recycling List for Today

_____
_____
_____
_____
_____
_____
_____
_____
_____
_____
_____

Today I Love Earth Because...

_____
_____
_____

How Did I Reduce my Waste Today?

_____
_____
_____
_____

Recycle 'Love Earth'

DATE: _____

How did I Help The Environment Today?

☐

☐

☐

☐

☐

☐

What Can I Re-use?

_____
_____
_____
_____
_____
_____
_____
_____

My Recycling List for Today

_____
_____
_____
_____
_____
_____
_____
_____
_____
_____

Today I Love Earth Because...

_____
_____
_____

How Did I Reduce my Waste Today?

_____
_____
_____
_____

Recycle

'Love Earth'

DATE: _____

How did I Help The Environment Today?

☐

☐

☐

☐

☐

☐

Today I Love Earth Because...

What Can I Re-use?

My Recycling List for Today

How Did I Reduce my Waste Today?

Recycle

'Love Earth'

DATE: _____

How did I Help The Environment Today?

☐

☐

☐

☐

☐

☐

What Can I Re-use?

_____
_____
_____
_____
_____
_____
_____
_____

My Recycling List for Today

_____
_____
_____
_____
_____
_____
_____
_____
_____
_____

Today I Love Earth Because...

_____
_____
_____

How Did I Reduce my Waste Today?

_____
_____
_____
_____

 **Recycle** 'Love Earth'

DATE: _____

How did I Help The Environment Today?

What Can I Re-use?

_____
_____
_____
_____
_____
_____
_____

My Recycling List for Today

_____
_____
_____
_____
_____
_____
_____

Today I Love Earth Because...

_____
_____
_____

How Did I Reduce my Waste Today?

_____
_____
_____
_____

Recycle 'Love Earth'

DATE: _____

How did I Help The Environment Today?

☐

☐

☐

☐

☐

☐

What Can I Re-use?

_____
_____
_____
_____
_____
_____
_____

My Recycling List for Today

_____
_____
_____
_____
_____
_____
_____
_____

Today I Love Earth Because...

_____
_____
_____

How Did I Reduce my Waste Today?

_____
_____
_____
_____

Recycle

'Love Earth'

DATE: _____

How did I Help The Environment Today?

- [ ]
- [ ]
- [ ]
- [ ]
- [ ]
- [ ]

Today I Love Earth Because...

What Can I Re-use?

My Recycling List for Today

How Did I Reduce my Waste Today?

 'Love Earth'

DATE: _____

How did I Help The Environment Today?

☐

☐

☐

☐

☐

☐

Today I Love Earth Because...

_____

_____

_____

What Can I Re-use?

_____
_____
_____
_____
_____
_____
_____
_____

My Recycling List for Today

_____
_____
_____
_____
_____
_____
_____
_____
_____
_____

How Did I Reduce my Waste Today?

_____
_____
_____
_____

 'Love Earth'

DATE: _____

How did I Help The Environment Today?

What Can I Re-use?

☐

☐

☐

☐

☐

☐

Today I Love Earth Because...

My Recycling List for Today

How Did I Reduce my Waste Today?

 'Love Earth'

DATE: _____

How did I Help The Environment Today?

What Can I Re-use?

_____
_____
_____
_____
_____
_____
_____
_____

My Recycling List for Today

_____
_____
_____
_____
_____
_____
_____
_____
_____
_____
_____
_____

Today I Love Earth Because...

_____
_____
_____

How Did I Reduce my Waste Today?

_____
_____
_____
_____

Recycle

'Love Earth'

D A T E: _____

How did I Help The Environment Today?

☐

☐

☐

☐

☐

☐

Today I Love Earth Because...

_____
_____
_____

What Can I Re-use?

_____
_____
_____
_____
_____
_____
_____

My Recycling List for Today

_____
_____
_____
_____
_____
_____
_____
_____
_____

How Did I Reduce my Waste Today?

_____
_____
_____
_____

Recycle

'Love Earth'

DATE: _____

How did I Help The Environment Today?

☐

☐

☐

☐

☐

☐

Today I Love Earth Because...

_____

_____

_____

What Can I Re-use?

_____
_____
_____
_____
_____
_____
_____

My Recycling List for Today

_____
_____
_____
_____
_____
_____
_____
_____
_____
_____

How Did I Reduce my Waste Today?

_____
_____
_____
_____

 'Love Earth'

DATE: _____

How did I Help The Environment Today?

What Can I Re-use?

_____
_____
_____
_____
_____
_____
_____
_____

My Recycling List for Today

_____
_____
_____
_____
_____
_____
_____
_____

Today I Love Earth Because...

_____
_____
_____

_____
_____
_____
_____
_____

How Did I Reduce my Waste Today?

_____
_____
_____
_____

 'Love Earth'

D A T E: _____

How did I Help The Environment Today?

What Can I Re-use?

- [ ]
- [ ]
- [ ]
- [ ]
- [ ]
- [ ]

My Recycling List for Today

Today I Love Earth Because...

How Did I Reduce my Waste Today?

 'Love Earth'

DATE: _____

How did I Help The Environment Today?

☐

☐

☐

☐

☐

☐

Today I Love Earth Because...

_____
_____
_____

What Can I Re-use?

_____
_____
_____
_____
_____
_____
_____

My Recycling List for Today

_____
_____
_____
_____
_____
_____
_____
_____
_____

How Did I Reduce my Waste Today?

_____
_____
_____
_____

 'Love Earth'

DATE: _____

How did I Help The Environment Today?

What Can I Re-use?

☐

☐

☐

☐

☐

☐

My Recycling List for Today

Today I Love Earth Because...

How Did I Reduce my Waste Today?

Recycle

'Love Earth'

DATE: _____

How did I Help The Environment Today?

☐

☐

☐

☐

☐

☐

What Can I Re-use?

_____
_____
_____
_____
_____
_____
_____
_____
_____
_____

My Recycling List for Today

_____
_____
_____
_____
_____
_____
_____
_____
_____
_____
_____
_____
_____

Today I Love Earth Because...

_____
_____
_____

How Did I Reduce my Waste Today?

_____
_____
_____
_____

Recycle

'Love Earth'

DATE: _____

How did I Help The Environment Today?

☐

☐

☐

☐

☐

☐

Today I Love Earth Because...

_____

_____

_____

What Can I Re-use?

_____
_____
_____
_____
_____
_____
_____
_____

My Recycling List for Today

_____
_____
_____
_____
_____
_____
_____
_____
_____
_____
_____

How Did I Reduce my Waste Today?

_____
_____
_____
_____

Recycle

'Love Earth'

DATE: _____

How did I Help The Environment Today?

- [ ]
- [ ]
- [ ]
- [ ]
- [ ]
- [ ]

What Can I Re-use?

_____
_____
_____
_____
_____
_____
_____
_____
_____
_____

My Recycling List for Today

_____
_____
_____
_____
_____
_____
_____
_____
_____
_____
_____
_____

Today I Love Earth Because...

_____
_____
_____

How Did I Reduce my Waste Today?

_____
_____
_____
_____

 'Love Earth'

DATE: _____

How did I Help The Environment Today?

☐

☐

☐

☐

☐

☐

Today I Love Earth Because...

_____
_____
_____

What Can I Re-use?

_____
_____
_____
_____
_____
_____
_____

My Recycling List for Today

_____
_____
_____
_____
_____
_____
_____
_____
_____

How Did I Reduce my Waste Today?

_____
_____
_____
_____

Recycle

'Love Earth'

DATE: _____

How did I Help The Environment Today?

☐

☐

☐

☐

☐

☐

Today I Love Earth Because...

_____

_____

_____

What Can I Re-use?

_____
_____
_____
_____
_____
_____
_____
_____

My Recycling List for Today

_____
_____
_____
_____
_____
_____
_____
_____
_____

How Did I Reduce my Waste Today?

_____
_____
_____
_____

Recycle

'Love Earth'

DATE: _____

How did I Help The Environment Today?

☐

☐

☐

☐

☐

☐

What Can I Re-use?

_____
_____
_____
_____
_____
_____
_____
_____
_____

My Recycling List for Today

_____
_____
_____
_____
_____
_____
_____
_____
_____
_____

Today I Love Earth Because...

_____
_____
_____

How Did I Reduce my Waste Today?

_____
_____
_____
_____

Recycle

'Love Earth'

DATE: _____

How did I Help The Environment Today?

☐

☐

☐

☐

☐

☐

Today I Love Earth Because...

_____
_____
_____

What Can I Re-use?

_____
_____
_____
_____
_____
_____
_____
_____

My Recycling List for Today

_____
_____
_____
_____
_____
_____
_____
_____
_____
_____

How Did I Reduce my Waste Today?

_____
_____
_____
_____

 'Love Earth'

DATE: _____

How did I Help The Environment Today?

What Can I Re-use?

_____
_____
_____
_____
_____
_____
_____
_____

My Recycling List for Today

_____
_____
_____
_____
_____
_____
_____
_____
_____
_____

Today I Love Earth Because...

_____
_____
_____

How Did I Reduce my Waste Today?

_____
_____
_____
_____

Recycle 'Love Earth'

DATE: _____

How did I Help The Environment Today?

☐

☐

☐

☐

☐

☐

Today I Love Earth Because...

_____
_____
_____

What Can I Re-use?

_____
_____
_____
_____
_____
_____
_____
_____

My Recycling List for Today

_____
_____
_____
_____
_____
_____
_____
_____
_____
_____

How Did I Reduce my Waste Today?

_____
_____
_____
_____

Recycle
'Love Earth'
DATE: _____

How did I Help The Environment Today?

☐

☐

☐

☐

☐

☐

What Can I Re-use?

_____
_____
_____
_____
_____
_____
_____

My Recycling List for Today

_____
_____
_____
_____
_____
_____
_____
_____
_____
_____
_____

Today I Love Earth Because...

_____
_____
_____

How Did I Reduce my Waste Today?

_____
_____
_____
_____

 'Love Earth'

DATE: _____

How did I Help The Environment Today?

☐

☐

☐

☐

☐

☐

What Can I Re-use?

_____
_____
_____
_____
_____
_____
_____
_____
_____

My Recycling List for Today

_____
_____
_____
_____
_____
_____
_____
_____
_____
_____

Today I Love Earth Because...

_____
_____
_____

How Did I Reduce my Waste Today?

_____
_____
_____
_____
_____

Recycle  'Love Earth'

DATE: _____

How did I Help The Environment Today?

☐

☐

☐

☐

☐

☐

What Can I Re-use?

_____
_____
_____
_____
_____
_____
_____

My Recycling List for Today

_____
_____
_____
_____
_____
_____
_____
_____
_____
_____

Today I Love Earth Because...

_____
_____
_____

How Did I Reduce my Waste Today?

_____
_____
_____
_____

Recycle

'Love Earth'

DATE: _____

How did I Help The Environment Today?

☐

☐

☐

☐

☐

☐

Today I Love Earth Because...

_____
_____
_____

What Can I Re-use?

_____
_____
_____
_____
_____
_____
_____

My Recycling List for Today

_____
_____
_____
_____
_____
_____
_____
_____
_____
_____

How Did I Reduce my Waste Today?

_____
_____
_____
_____

 'Love Earth'

DATE: _____

How did I Help The Environment Today?

What Can I Re-use?

_____
_____
_____
_____
_____
_____
_____
_____
_____
_____

My Recycling List for Today

_____
_____
_____
_____
_____
_____
_____
_____
_____
_____
_____
_____

Today I Love Earth Because...

_____
_____
_____

How Did I Reduce my Waste Today?

_____
_____
_____
_____